LAPIDARY

Also by Richard Marx Weinraub

Wonder Bread Hill
San Juan, PR: University of Puerto Rico Press, 2002

Heavenly Bodies
Hoboken, NJ: Poets Wear Prada, 2008

Maravilla Rebanada
Translated by Elidio La Torre Lagares
San Juan, PR: Terranova Editores, 2009

LAPIDARY

Richard Marx Weinraub

POETS WEAR PRADA • Hoboken, New Jersey

Lapidary

Copyright © 2013 Richard Marx Weinraub

All rights reserved. Except for use in any review or for educational purposes, the reproduction or utilization of this work in whole or in part in any form by electronic, mechanical or other means, now known or hereafter invented, including xerography, photocopying and recording, or in any informational or retrieval system, is forbidden without the written permission of the publisher:

> Poets Wear Prada
> 533 Bloomfield Street, Second Floor
> Hoboken, New Jersey 07030
> http://pwpbooks.blogspot.com

First North American Publication 2013
First Mass Market Paperback Edition 2013

Grateful acknowledgment is made to the following publications where some of these poems have appeared or are forthcoming:

> *Asheville Poetry Review*, *A Bad Penny Review*, *Big Pulp*, *Black Lantern*, *Blast Furnace*, *The Brownstone Poets 2012 Anthology* (Patricia Carragon), *Buddhist Poetry Review*, *Danse Macabre*, "Divine Intimacy," *Eye to the Telescope*, *Green Briar Review*, *Iambs & Trochees*, *Impractical Cats* (Medusa's Laugh Press), *Oyez Review*, *Penguin Review*, *Up the Staircase Quarterly*, *The Waiting Room Reader II* (CavanKerry Press), and *VQ*.

ISBN-13: 978-0615833224
ISBN-10: 0615833225

Library of Congress Control Number: 2013910835

Printed in the U.S.A.

Cover Design: Roxanne Hoffman
Author Photo: Carnival Cruise Lines

*In memory of my father,
I. R. Weinraub*

Table of Contents

Marble	3
Aquamarine	4
Ruby	6
Smokey Quartz	7
White Topaz	8
Padparadscha	9
Star Sapphire	11
Citrine	12
Emerald	13
Amethyst	14
Diamond	15
Cubic Zirconium	17
Amber	18
Flint	20
Jasper	22
Garnet	23
Onyx	25
Zircon	26
Apache Tears	28
Copal	29
Opal	30
Rock Crystal	32
Created Sapphire	33
Peridot	34
Jet	35
Lapis Lazuli	36

Doublet	*37*
Goshenite	*38*
Moonstone	*39*
Bloodstone	*40*
Lodestone	*41*
Rose Quartz	*42*
Pearl	*43*
Coral	*44*
Ivory	*45*
Cat's Eye	*46*
Cornelian	*47*
Tanzanite	*49*
Agate	*50*
Helenite	*51*
Alexandrite	*53*
Spinel	*55*
Turquoise	*56*
Nephrite	*57*
Jade	*58*

Acknowledgments
About the Author

LAPIDARY

... when I try to imagine a faultless love
Or the life to come, what I hear is the murmur
Of underground streams, what I see is a limestone landscape.

— W.H. Auden, "In Praise of Limestone"

Marble

Imagine your love is Venus de Milo —
but whole — come to life in your living room.
Her alabaster cast has turned back to olive;
she is eighteen — younger than Empire —
and pure — for she came before Christ.

Now picture this woman (who's not quite a woman,
but a child conceived in your fantasy)
just sits there in front of your living room window
turning clouds into nimbus — your tool to a chisel —
as you make her — the image of God.

She's not God exactly — but the rock of your vision
as it pinches her small milkless breasts —
and parts her — with tresses of marble — and lashes
her buttocks so hard that you feel like a man
who can forge a new world out of stone.

Her Vulcanized lover — you're thrown out of Heaven
and fall — for her morning and eve.
You're deformed — while she twists in a natural manner
away from you — hours a pop
coming back to your niche with pricks in her arms.

Imagine you kiss your impassive creation
and bitterness shudders your frame.
The smack that addicted you to her is yours,
so you're losing your marbles detaching her arms
to be mortar in Love's subterrain.

Aquamarine

I weighed two hundred forty pounds
but I was never blue —
just glaucous like my precious little sister —
created by the Amazon
of northwestern Brazil —
vainglorious from the umbilical.

Macadam — eave — and adamant
unearthed me from the womb;
the lapidary cut me with his saw.
The fire in the devil's oven
broke my iron will —
my greenness stolen, as he made me blue.

And now my aqua covers up
a stronger, jealous grain,
and my marine makes war upon the emerald,
bombarding her with pointed gems
that cut the mother lode —
reducing me to brittle, brilliant stones.

The needle brilliant and the star
reflect what I have lost —
still — cut to bits — I know how large I am.
When turned aside I capture light,
I didn't know in earth,
exhibiting a greater green in blue.

And so unnatural as I am
I'm perfect for your world —
just put my tablet in a bowl of aqua
and stare until you lose yourself

beneath the glaucous Earth
consuming vitae with the weight of me.

Ruby

They call me Ruby — but I hate my name;
it sounds like I'm cheap — not dear like Amour.
Red sapphire's better — or carmine corundum —
for I am Romance — a crimson conundrum.

They call me: "Ruby!" — as if I'm a babe,
but I am so hard — and I don't have cleavage.
I show them desired directions of parting
though sometimes they break me while cutting and setting.

They called me Ruby, the Hermaphrodite;
Greeks wore me at sea with my arms round their necks.
Used by the flesh, I am blood-gorged and male;
neglected, I turn to a maiden and pale.

They call in Ruby when the scales have been tipped —
when the seamen are wrong in the head,
for I am the line joining pigeon and blood —
the purple propelling the fish to the dove.

Smokey Quartz

The soothing cigarette that leaves
The passerby infirm
The barbeque that makes the pig
Delicious — and the worm
The smoke and mirrors in the house
The smoke screen that's homespun
The fat cigar in Monica
The lawyer's smoking gun
The burning of the midnight oil
That fills your world with strife
The remnants of the shot that killed
The man who raped your wife
The smoke of the electric chair
The fire from Aaron's rod
Both ends of tallow candles burned
To conjure a pure God
The rock of your morality
The value of my face
A cross between ashes and snuff
The color of the human race

White Topaz

A Boer from *nether* lands — I'm bored and boring —
my cleavage: perfect — fools think I'm a diamond.
I'm number one — America's favorite gemstone.
I'm on the TV — Quality Value Convenience.

I'm easy to get — I'm poetry for the masses.
I'm in the hands and on the hearts of millions —
objectified and hot — I come in colors.

It's smart to take vacations from your visage.
Topazos in the Red Sea is Zebirget.
My greatest fear is I'll revert to nature —
my glory in the past — now that is boring.

Saint Hildegarde used me on the people's blindness —
she put me in a glass of wine — Teutonic —
they rubbed me on their eyes then drank the tincture.
But when they tried me on the plague — bubonic —
I didn't do the trick — it was disgusting.

Now I am in an epic made by Ezra —
the eyes in his "Medallion," turned to topaz,
when wedded with technology, producing
half-witted, half-watt rays — it doesn't work.

Padparadscha

My mother rock, a dolomitized limestone,
was violated by the windlass hoist.
In Sinhalese, the "mine" of man is *illam*
so what was mine becomes an iliad.
Gestation is backbreaking in Sri Lanka.

I'm given definition by the Tamils —
black, almost naked men who slave for me.
I'm picked and loosened — carried off in baskets
precipitated from enfolding clay —
I'm agitated in the Mahaweli.

The wise old saw has teeth — the teeth of diamonds;
I'm put upon — a copper spinning wheel —
a Ceylon cut — and buffed by straps of leather —
a piece accomplished on the fiddle bow
transfiguring the piercing flame of Nero

I come to light — the golden Padparadscha —
the only sapphire having a first name.
In Sinhalese, it means the "lotus flower,"
the yellow lily with Homeric leaves
which gather up the sun out of the water.

Colombo is the jewel of the ocean,
but I am all that was before Colón.
Forget about the past — I have the fire
of spirit filtered through the verdant world —
verbena, cinnamon, and citronella.

And so I take the shape of my Sri Lanka —
sometimes I am a mango or a pear —

sometimes I am a teardrop — in Nirvana —
you have to have a form to see through there —
and I am it — the body which is precious.

However, when two peoples of my island,
the Sinhalese and Indian Tamils,
use fire to destroy each other's colors
I change into the lotus jujubee
and want to eat myself and purge reflection

but turn instead to pages of the Sutra,
the Lotus of the Most Wonderful Law,
and emanate the teachings of the Buddha
that every human being rides the wind
upon the Earth — and Earth's the Padparadscha.

Star Sapphire

Found among the roots of the Hindu world tree
Worn around the necks of the Kings from the East
Protecting the Magi from Satan and God
Sapphic star sapphire

Fathers of the Church once thought I was sacred
Now I am scared seeing into Earth's spirit
Brothers of Christ do not look straight to me with
Crooks in their pupils

Filled with titanium — barren as Sarah
Rounding me off — I'm your six-pointed aster
Loving means always — but if you're not true I
Will turn midnight blue

Citrine

Gentlemen prefer blonde Crystals
Like that bitch in *Dynasty*
Fake and cheap, it doesn't matter
Honey sometimes; lemon always
I will make you pucker up
Marvelous upon the finger
Mansfield   Marilyn   Madonna
Rose of Sharon turned to Stone
I am quartz — in Slavic, "hard"
What is hard opens the heart
Channel to the Holy Spirit
Powering the Pleiades' ship
I am *As You Like It*'s Touchstone
Singing out the Truth in drag
Clearing mucus from the larynx
Billy Crystal loves me only
For the moment like Apollo
What this world needs now is Stones
Dusty Springfield — teams of fruit flies
Goddessly, gentles, I tell you
Be fruits and don't multiply!

Emerald

Your irides are green; I know you well.
I see all that's included in your eyes:
the feathers of you — fissures, rents, and splits —
the fractures that you suffered as a child —
the titan oxidized beneath your skin —
crude lipids of another lodged within.

So you have flaws — clear is the water's realm;
my sister Aqua's perfect — but not rare.
Your imperfections are a garden
green — your fallen nature — just the hue of life.
So what if you are bitter — bile is sweet
when it breaks down the animals you eat.

I'm just like you — digesting minerals —
beryllium, aluminum, and chrome —
originating in a fault of earth;
I grew my veins on walls of cavities.
And so I have resource to read your mind
for also I am neither cruel nor kind.

I hear the sea, the heavens, and the dead
within a tone described as *smáragdos*
by natives of the Islands of the Blessed
where emerald builds the Temples of the Gods.
I see a human being that's depressed,
but in your temples I'm at your behest.

Amethyst

I have the flavor of the sweetest wine
I'm *a methystos* — "not dead drunk" in Greek
Protecting those devoted to the vine

The Jews used me to conquer Palestine
My kiddush cup was filled with God's mystique
I had the flavor of the sweetest wine

Egyptians cut me into cats and kine
To catch the soul of what they could not seek
Protecting those devoted to the vine

For Christian fathers purple was a sign
That Christ was here and through them He would speak
I have the flavor of the sweetest wine

For crystal gazers I will undermine
The power of the rabbi, pope, and sheik
Protecting those devoted to the vine

If dropped into pure water in a stein
And bathed in sunlight during Holy Week
I have the flavor of the sweetest wine
Protecting those devoted from the Vine

Diamond

Adamas, "the unconquerable,"
Adonis-like, but God-damned hard,
I lived with the most awful king —
the cold Tyrannosaurus rex —
compressed into a world of coal
and turned a millionfold to ice.

Volcanic pipes throw up the ice
I thought was so unconquerable
as I am ripped away from coal
blue ground. I'm crushed. Christ, it is hard.
A giant Caterpillar wrecks
the Rock I was for a new king.

My soul is studied by the king —
three kings — who peer through panes of ice
deciding where to cut. They're wrecks
absorbing the unconquerable
till they finally brute me — hard —
and I'm just tar and feathers — coal

upon the Southern Cross — the Coal
sack turned to features of a king
as I am ground against the hard
edge of myself by one of ice.
He thinks he's so unconquerable
and knows the way to raise the wrecks.

I'm put, forever, by some Rex
on some Regina from the coal
country so he's unconquerable

like the old Adam or the King
in Shakespeare's *Winter's Tale*: the ice
inflating man (kind) to be hard.

But when he is no longer hard —
just adamant and cruel — he wrecks
the marriage and she dabs some ice
upon her face. Putting Nat Cole
and Elvis on, she thanks the King —
for I remain — unconquerable.

Unconquerable's too God-damned hard,
and kingdom come is filled with wrecks.
Play me Cole Porter — that will break the ice.

Cubic Zirconium

My diamond imitation's true
because the blushing bride and groom
are rung with what will prove too real —
inviolable bands — till death.

Attachment is the seed of death.
But as the golden bells ring true,
"altar" means "stable" to the groom;
"nave" winds the bride upon a reel.

The swoon of marriage is a reel;
the life within her — certain death.
His bank account is out of true —
but he's a lawyer she can groom.

While pongids serve the group they groom,
men think monogamy is real;
this fakery will be the death
of them, as man-made dreams come true.

Amber

I am the living tears of the Heliades,
the daughters of the Sun turned into poplar trees.
The palace of the Sun was lit by brilliant gems;
the time was always high noon — too bright for humans.
Half-mortal Phaëthon, however, belled the cat
approaching the gold throne where Helios has sat
through time. The mother of the boy had told her son
Helios was his father, but his friends bought none
of this — so he was there to bring to light the truth.
The Sun took off his burning crown and told the youth,
"Clymene's right — and I will give you anything
to show you, Phaëthon, you are the Sun's offspring."
Since Phaëthon had seen the Sun God's steeds go far
and wide, "For just one day I want to drive your car,"
the young man cried. The Sun was horrified at this;
he heard the longing of his son become a hiss,
but nothing could dissuade his golden, steadfast son.
So when Dawn opened up her court and stars had run
their course, the gates of Mt. Olympus were agape;
a diamond rope yoked horse to driver by the nape,
and Phaëthon controlled his father's burnished car.
Ecstatic, son became the Sun — a mortal star.
The carriage went so fast the wind was left behind.
He flew the coupe to Heaven leaving humankind.
Young Phaëthon pronounced himself Lord of the Sky.
But when the car swung to-and-fro, to rectify
his course he drove the steeds cruelly — losing control.
The weight the horses felt in back was a black hole.
Accustomed to the Sun's light touch threading the Conch,
each beast of burden turned into a bucking bronc.
They weaved their way through Scorpio then hit the Bull;
the reins that Phaëthon had cracked were hard to pull.

They soared up to the solar vault. When they plunged down
the world was set on fire. From Gaea's highest crown,
Olympus, to the valleys — rivers turned to steam.
The Nile fled and hid the head which was a stream.
Repentantly, he wept flambeaus for what he burned,
and even Zeus — cold-hearted God — became concerned.
And so He hurled a thunderbolt and killed the son
as Phaëthon rained from the sky on everyone.
The River of Eridanus received his corpse;
his sisters, the Heliades, still weep in warps
of time. As each tear falls into the water
a moment of the ancient past shines through me — amber.

Flint

See me
      Tunkashila
      the oldest of Gods
appear before everything
      everything ending
           but I
              never die

Lakotas are smart
they heed Tunkashila
producing gourd rattles
      from crystals
           of anthills

They pray
over rocks
in Montana
      for physics
to keep evil spirits
      at bay
           like George Custer

I speak through Yuwipi man*
      stone dreamer/writer
whose interlaced fingers
are bound round his spine
with the vellum of crow
      that he ate
           for safekeeping

He is covered with stars
He is wrapped like a mummy

He is laid on his face
in some
        sage
Spirits use him

Spirits suck out the light
almost suck out his life
        until *Tunka wasichun*†
            reincarnates
the raven

It's the lightning of me
the sparks flying
        from flint
as the moon
        knocks against
            planet Earth

            It's the lightning that frees
the Yuwipi man's fear
of the darkness of death
        your disease

* medicine man or healer
† rock power

Jasper

A little stone, *iaspis*, found inside the head
of *aspis*, I am the body's antibody —
coagulated spirit on top of the spine —
beginning with the daughter of the Universe.
As she went walking through her favorite garden
and heard loud drumming coming from beneath a tree,
she started digging what became a giant hole.
Stumbling in, she spiraled hellbent down the sky.
Earthly beings at that time were very soft.
They inhabited the Spiral's depths without the spark
of thought — floating in the waters of the world.

The Great Matter seeing His only daughter drop
implored the creatures of the Earth to mitigate
her plop. They turned their eyes to see a falling star,
and thinking it a gift from God, created ways
to cushion her. The Turtle offered up its back —
the Snake its skin. The Water Spider and Muskrat
dove deep within the blue, and brought up spongy loam
to envelope the planet's shell. The Buzzard made
the jagged ground grow soft with grass and gossamer.

Star Woman hurtled towards the sea, but Earth caught her.
Her grateful tears sprang lakes and streams of fresh water:
this world — the Turtle Island of the Cherokee —
sown with stones from the welkin's womb — aventurine
and chalcedony — for her saviors' sustenance.
I was devoured by the Serpent and despised
because I lay on Cleopatra's poisoned breast.
I'm what's the matter and the matter's antidote —
a city made of jasper — New Jerusalem —
imagination eating what its entrails spew.

Garnet

Make sacrifices to me:
I am your fetish.
The Bghai tribe of Burma
understood my power;
they offered me fresh blood
so I would not eat them.

I am the color of lips
consumed by fever
or beautified by wax
instilled with pigment —
crushed female bodies,
kermes or cochineal.

Rubescence of swollen tits
will satisfy me —
the cherub satiated
and then the sandman.
But soon desire awakens
and the jewel beckons.

For forty days and nights,
Noah watched me glisten;
the only sun he had —
was a bloody dragon.
Obsessively he gaped,
as I turned to Allah.

In bullets of Kashmir
and the cut carbuncle,
I am the wound itself —
Jesus on the rood-tree

in cabochon —
the head of the *tallis* man.

Onyx

Even the Hellenes — those swarthy satyrs —
disliked what they nicknamed the dark *fingernail*.
Their chromatics revealed
black's the father of all,
so in jealousy they made me horny.

They inlaid me with white capricorni
cavorting amidst evergreen myrtle trees.
They spread through the grapevines
that anyone who wore me
would know sable visions, ebony dreams.

But I've had the nightmares — of being in chains,
of being sealed up in white rings,
so men would caress me for hardness and power
and use the dark *claw* to dissever sweet hearts.

Zircon

I exhibit dispersion
I am dense and amorphous
I am brilliant and sensitive to knocks
I am confused

with demantoid
and cubic zirconium
A rose by any other
would still entreat

I've forgotten — my
name? "They called me
the hyacinth girl"‡
Hyacinth? (Gladiolus? Larkspur? Or Iris?)

Jacinth? Or Starlight? Jargoon? (Is it Jargon?)
Did I come from the Persian? Old French? Middle English?
From *gargle*? Or *gargoyle*?
A throat? Or the gutter?

Was I hit by a discus?
From Apollo? From Zephyr?
I remember — I forget ...
(I was mixed with uranium

some thorium — then laudanum)
... the rockrose of Israel
and then by the Abbess
with a hot cross of Bread

casting stones from the Devil
of madness she said

Was my psyche cast too?
Or was I the discus?

‡ T.S. Eliot, *The Waste Land*, New York: Horace Liveright, 1922

Apache Tears

Upon the steppes of Kilimanjaro
I watched successive hominids arise
from Tanzania's fructuous plateau
evaporating in sulfurous skies
so hot they cut the serpent down to size
and made a worm out of the millipede
diminishing within the leopard's eyes
I weep volcanic tears for Adam's seed

Man snaked his way up rivers to Bordeaux
and ogled humans with a different guise
seducing them until an epic snow
killed game. Cro-Magnon man did not despise
Neanderthals but had to improvise
repasts. He hunted them until their breed
was gone — then covered up his shame with lies
I weep volcanic tears for Adam's seed

Man walked on waters of a great ice floe
across the frozen gulf to humanize
the other world. He went to Mexico
and worshipped an obsidian so wise
it still reflects the images he scries
demanding fantasy be done in deed
the beating heart outside the man who dies
I weep volcanic tears for Adam's seed

Though man is fruitful as he multiplies
digesting what he views in the black bead
he hears extinguished past and future cries
I weep volcanic tears for Adam's seed

Copal

She tightly pulls the noose around her neck
and feels the fastening of fossil balls.
Her heart is in her throat; it sounds my beck
and call. Her skin is serpentine and crawls
to me. The collar begs to be a ring.

Her eyes have turned luciferous. The source
is undulating on a leather string:
an Aztec copal serpent carved by force.

And force's random hand determined how
the forests wept a million years ago
entombing seeds and insects in the slough
creating witness to the living now.

The resin on this rag preserves her so
she will abide by me, her Lord, in tow.

Opal

Selfish people fear what's marvelous
casting it as aberrant or strange
preaching holy ones come from the Deuce
giving crystal balls the evil eye

Institutions pan the harlequin
making cabbage out of my *caboche*
Roundheads, churches, synagogues, and mosques
metamorphose fire to prejudice

Language formulates a pigeonhole
"opal" changed to "ophal" by the Queen
saying it made flesh invisible
calling it the touchstone of true thieves

Walter Scott put opal in the hair
of the vampirish Hermione
giving me a necromantic air
sparkling when the sorceress was gay

shooting out red rays when she was mad
till an aspergillum saved the day
sprinkling holy water over me
turning what was brilliant into dust

Nature's book, however, tells the truth
(aided by the science of the glass)
microscopic spheres in silicon
cause the iridescence of my face

I am Iris bowing over Earth
looking into irises of babes

burning with the colors of my play
you will cure the illness of your I

Rock Crystal

Crows gathered my oscillations
To make them hover
For Hindus I was Maya's work
A tank of water
Greeks thought I was eternal ice
So called me "crystal"

The Japanese named me "hard breath"
Of the White Dragon
A symbol of infinity
And perseverance
Making a perfect sphere of me
With just a hammer

Subjecting me to cast iron
Nippon's great grinder
Turned me and turned me
On the wheel applying garnet
Polishing me perpetually
With rouge and crocus

But now I'm in the factories
Of Yokohama
Inserted automatically
In Sharp® timepieces
The universal frequency
Reduced to ticking

Created Sapphire

There's a sapphire in his loveseat.
It fell through pearl cushions and into the pit
beneath the fabric of the winding sheet.

The color of inkling, the shape of a teat,
its brilliance disperses from where he sits.
There's a sapphire in his loveseat.

Created artificially in heat,
it mirrors bunnies, bread, and what was writ
beneath the fabric of the winding sheet.

When they have tabled him with rigid feet
and analyzed his entrails they will spit:
"There's a sapphire in his loveseat!

"There's a sapphire in his loveseat
beneath the fabric of the winding-sheet."

Peridot

I fell to the Earth from a shooting star,
landing on Zabargad or Serpent Island.
The Crusaders thought I came from the Sun
and called me *chrysolite* — blind to my colors.
They carted me, mule-back, to a church in Cologne
and stowed me in the Magi's treasury.

They carved an image of a mule upon me
hoping their future would so be divined,
but all I could ken was sterility —
their civilization built on my back,
their spinning machines changing cotton to gold,
with smugglers and pirates running amok.

Endowed with power to dispel demons,
while man seemed the very devil himself —
stringing me up with pointed fingers —
I am done being pressured for tricks
I can't reproduce. Let me be beached
on the olivine sands of the Dragon.

Jet

Helenus wrapped me in Hector's swaddle,
fasting for twenty-one days to augur
Zeus's decree in desire's battle,
leeching the Greeks and the weary Trojans.

Helenus offered me sacrifices:
all he consumed on a daily basis —
partridges, pottages, pigs, and pastries —
heaping on me what sustained his people.

Begging the babe in his arms to suck him,
emptying everything lodged within him,
asking the future to fill the vacuum,
Helenus ate me and heaved his vision.

What could I show him except my nature?
Volatile carbon from Oltu, Turkey;
earthwork of Troy sown with flames of velvet
thrown by the prophet — like Hector's baby.

Lapis Lazuli
After Yeats

I have heard hysterical laureates say
They are sick of the way people pigeonhole
Poets as being always gay,
For laureates know the rigmarole
Poëphobes use to write them off
Understanding their brethren who do come out
Are treated as if they have whooping cough
Or worse, they are jailed and become devout.

All perform legerdemain:
There struts Melville, there is Yeats,
That's Anne Sexton, that Mark Twain;
Yet should they be knocking at lapis gates,
The eye of the peacock about to close,
They finally try on the other's array
And do not snort their lines and pose —
They know that Melville and Yeats are gay.

The eyes of King Tut and the Moon God Sin
Are lined with lapis lazuli;
Each scarab of truth has a faint heart within
Becoming a symbol of poetry.
Inscribed on these hearts is the Book of the Dead
Dedicated to the Sun God Re;
When he places these ornaments on his head,
His eyes, his ancient glittering eyes, are gay.

Doublet

You see me on the street, a cherry heart;
my table's set for you to feast upon.
You know you've found the real thing — finally —

affordably — for, say, two hundred bucks —
not bad for booty — I mean a ruby
laid in the Golden Mile of San Juan.

You have so many syns. from which to choose —
so many fakes dressed up in diamond drag:
there's YAG (real name: Yttrium A. Garnet)

and Galliant (GGG in the trade);
there's Boule that drips as cradles incarn it —
but only I am art — desire's slag.

My seamless face reflects cohesiveness;
the king's corundum and the people's quartz
are fused in me with a glue of scarlet —

my clear pavilion crimsoned by my crown.
Call me your love or call me a harlot;
reality is what the heart distorts.

Goshenite

Precious beryl, a colorless emerald,
I'm from Goshen, a region in Egypt,
or, if you prefer, Massachusetts,
the garden before the green journey.

I appear in the book (not the movie)
Exodus — on the High Priest of Israel
in the breastplate of judgment with cunning —
in row four next to onyx and jasper.

I was cut in the shape of an apple,
and engraved with four letters of YHWH.
Forbidden to utter the real name of God,
four seraphim ruling four planets were carved.

I was used by John Dee for soothsaying,
and he saw Mary's death in my crystal —
the ascent of the new moon, the Virgin —
the bloody garden before the green journey.

Moonstone
For Queen Elizabeth I

My family is Feldspar
    "the split field"
        in German
I'm made of right
    Angles
        their flag on the moon

My dome has the bluish
    fluorescence of lovers
Inside of their mouths
    I can soothsay
        the horn

My luster is argent
    I make people
        looney
The Baron of Bulbeck
    saw phases
        in me

A shade in the crown
    in the shape of a cradle
        moved down to my middle
    increased
        red and full

Turned back through the top
    of the head
        young King Edward
        was dead
    and the *feld spar*
demanded the Moon

Bloodstone

As long as you hold me — in reverence —
whatever you want I will grant you.
Are you old? I will green you with hornblende.
If you're pink you'll be ruddled with iron.

Just put me in water and watch it
turn red like a blood revelation.
If you're frightened and faithfully drink it
you will see a dead man's resurrection.

And when you're concerned for the nation
and carve the right verses upon me
I will tear through the bindings that hurt you.
I will break down the walls that invert you.

Berlin and the wall of your wailing
were prisons that led into freedom.
I will open the door into Heaven
for the body is made out of stone.

Lodestone

I'm so attractive Earth thinks I'm her lover:
in Chinese I'm *t'su shi*, "loving stone" —
in Sanskrit I'm *chumbaka*, "the great kisser."

But Plato was the first to use my substance
to fashion myths — to lighten up the cave —
bringing to Earth the lodestar to lead the way.

On Mount Ida, a shepherd, Magnes, found me
attached to nails protruding from his sole —
so today what has pull is called "magnetic."

The Roman priests formed Venus from my blackness
then made an iron monument of Mars.
Drawn by the unseen universal power

the God of War flew to his antipode —
as Nature unifies her disparate members
if you will only bear the buried load.

Rose Quartz

You count on me to put you in the pink —
First mystery of joyful innocence
Delivered through my crystalline rosehips.
You tell the beads in fifty syllables
As decades slide away and God is born.

You think you've hit the nail upon the head
Because the second mystery's a cross
Between the white and red — the crowning thorns
That let His temples turn into a rose
You finger once again with bloody hands.

Hail Mary with the rosary in hand
Caressing just the black wool of the lamb
Without the genuflections of the past.
The final mystery's the answer found
Within the catechism: "I'm what rose."

Pearl

The mantle turns the irritating sands
of French society and English earls
into the brilliance of *The String of Pearls*
by wrapping nacre round the pricks in strands,
for pain's an impulse wisdom countermands,
as necklaces grow on the college girls
who dance the hula in volcanic swirls,
impelled by Washington with outstretched hands.
Without their *pearls of wisdom* they are "fish,"
a dish for Rockefeller's potency,
the shut and hard-to-open votary,
the means for men to capture every wish,
a shell a sandman takes into the arbor
to mount a fresh invasion of Pearl Harbor.

Coral

I make your world; I'm coupled with the brain,
snake, Gables, fungus, berry, bells, and Sea.
My afterlife is your applied domain
connected in one living colony.
Beginning in a cuplike cavity
I live as a medusa off Rincón;
my snaky polyps bud asexually
then turn the sunken garden into stone.
You make my sanguine skeleton your own
carving me into human figurines
calling me names like "angel skin" and "bone" —
afraid you'll break me into smithereens.
When you get sick and jealous I turn too;
we both come from the sea — my God — I'm you!

Ivory
A Tooth for a Tooth

Humanity has set my teeth on edge
equipped with buzz saw, chisel, rasp, and file.
Men pull me from the elephant and pledge
to build an ivory tower on the Nile
or in the Arctic Circle or the Sea
because I am the walrus, the "horse-whale,"
a species man has put in jeopardy,
creating low relief from God's travail.
And thinking I'm the holy unicorn
they bludgeon what's a corpse whale for the tusk,
the point of which the Inuits have borne
and suffered with upon the ivory dusk.
Man killed the mammoth and the mastodon —
so toothsome is this thought — he'll soon be gone.

Cat's Eye

I look just like a pussycat
but I am of another world
intent on catching the stonechat
I look just like a pussycat
chatoying with the vampire bat
with balls of knotty yarns uncurled
I look just like a pussycat
but I am of another world

Cornelian

Carved into an octagon,
I served as the blood of Isis;
dipped in juice of *ankhama*,
I preserved the flesh of the king.
Sycamore enveloped me
around the neck of his mummy.
(Horus joyed in seeing him
maintained for eternity.)

Centuries unwrapped the swathes,
as Muslims took over Egypt;
God, who'd been a bird and bull,
developed a human frame.
"Abraham, the slave of God"
was graved on my cherry crystal;
what had sealed eternity
was now just the master's seal.

Emperor Napoleon
took me when he marched through Egypt.
Imitating Anthony,
he meted out Roman law
wearing me on a watch chain
enslaved by the Sun God Amun.
I was passed on to his seed —
the second Napoleon.

Emperor Napoleon
the Third wore his uncle's fetish.
Losing France to Germany,
he willed the seal to his son.

Hanging me upon the Prince
and treating him as a mummy,
Africa reclaimed its blood
interring Cornelia's seed.

Tanzanite

As human beings rose up from the Gorge
I was created yellow, brown, and red
within the belly of the Maker's forge
invisible to the grasping biped.

I was created. Yellow, brown, and red
seafarers settled on my silicate
invisible to the grasping biped —
Azania became a sultanate.

Seafarers settled on my silicate —
the colors of the rainbow turned to blue.
Azania became a sultanate;
my spawn arrived in chains in Timbuktu.

The colors of the rainbow turned to blue
within the belly of the maker's forge.
My spawn arrived in chains in Timbuktu
as human beings rose up from the gorge.

Agate

Placed under a pillow, I bring good dreams —
I come from *Achates*, "the faithful friend";
Aeneas put geodes beneath his head
(in Crete after Troy was destroyed by flames)
and fancied his future — west Italy.

Achates's a river in Sicily,
the friend of the sailor who makes for Rome
escaping the Harpies — those reeking birds —
avoiding the straight and ensnaring pool
foreseen by the soothsaying Helenus.

But Juno, oppressed by the ways of Jove,
seduces with anger the King of Winds
who whips up a tempest and fags the cox
descending to Carthage with Neptune's pitch
till he's resurrected by Cupid's prick.

Aeneas is wrapped in the mist of Love —
Achates beside him — before the Queen
decked out to the nines with a train of slaves
increasing with time like the cars of Moon
till Venus, the mother, has saved the day.

Helenite

St. Helens
bloats
with embryonic gas

I push up
through her throat
with steam and mud

A massive crack
within her face
explodes

I'm out
to meet the world
It is a blast!

A lava
avalanche
creates my path

Engulfing
Woodland Cougar
and Spokane

The pumice
bleeds my mother
of her mass

It dams
the opening
to Spirit Lake

The rivers
boil
with pyroclastic flows

My magma cools
and quickly
turns to glass

In Portland
I am picked up
from the ash

And mounted
in a gallery
of gold

Alexandrite

I wish I could turn back the sun
and hide within the mother lode
having the value of the earth
not Russia's colors: red and green,

for people think I vacillate
like some chameleonic moon
reflecting patriotically
great Russia's colors: red and green.

Yes, I look celadon by day
and bay in artificial light,
but that's their iris — in and out —
not Russia's colors: red and green.

Yes, they discovered me the day
Prince Alexander turned thirteen,
but I was named after the fact
not Russia's colors: red and green.

Since history is retrospect
that petrifies the living play
creating premises for czars
and Russia's colors: red and green,

I have these lines — he sued for peace
and sold Alaska for a song
and died by an assassin's bomb
in Russia's colors: red and green —

but know he was responsible
in no small way for Lenin's rise

and Yeltsin's stoniness for I
am Russia's colors: red and green.

Spinel

The Ruby of the Black Prince? No! A thorn
in England's crown. Above the Lesser Star
of Africa — I've been mistaken — worn
by monarchs entertaining Zanzibar,
Chad, India, Australia, and Qatar.
I'm under lock and key in London's Tower
between the Scepters of the Dove and Cross —
I hear imprisoned sovereigns bell each hour —
engendered by His "Longshanks" — laid in dross —
I'm not a ruby — but an albatross.

Turquoise

The chattel of a Spanish gentleman, I lost my azure to his rouge, perfume, and sweat. The father of the Führer's doctor bought me for a trifling sum, and when he gave me to his son, I was as pale as high noon in Cologne. This owner, aptly named De Boot, believed the pallor of my face conveyed his father's phlegm. But when he graved his name on me and wore me on his finger, I turned Prussian blue! He said this showed affinity — when really it was just the German weather and costumery. While riding in a thunderstorm, his stallion threw him to the ground, but he sustained no broken bones; instead, I had absorbed the fall and broke in two. He was amazed my virtue was intact. Of course, he stabbed me in the back as men so often do. His *Treatise on the Turkish Stone* says, "Satan steals into the crone and makes you think she does what God can only do for you."

Nephrite

I'm *punamu*, the "green stone"
of the world's most acid place: New Zealand.
To find me, you must be of my own kidney

and journey to a barrow,
where the verdure is an organ pumping
waste out of your body. You are — in a trance —

tohunga, or "the wizard."
Anticipating death, you lie in earth
leading the living on the search for pureness.

You are your mother's body
and your father's pneuma enters quickly
directing you to serpentine deposits.

You tell your blood, Maoris,
where to dig and raise me from the stratum.
Eventually, you'll carve your father's spirit

and give it your expression,
putting in its eyes the mother-of-pearl
you'll wear in your *hei-tiki* on your bosom,

until you have been buried
by the son who takes me from your barrow
to purify your blood — now his — of poison.

Jade

Love comes in many forms, and I am love —
the *pao*, the "precious" character
configured as a house

holding an earthen jar, a shell, and beads.
All children in the household wear
a padlock made of me

protecting them from danger and disease.
And when young girls have come of age
I'm given as a bird

that rises from the ashes of its youth,
and then they have the butterflies
bestowed by handsome beaus

until the unicorn reveals its horn
conveying he who rides on top
with clicking castanets

has magic and an heir will soon be born.
The son will get an amulet
called Brothers of the Sky

depicting two strong men in an embrace.
Creating the divine intent
of planetary peace,

this precious pao, the poet's stone, is struck
so that the jade — the horse and whore —
resound in harmony.

Acknowledgments

The author extends his thanks to the editors of the following publications:

Asheville Poetry Review	"Marble"
A Bad Penny Review	"Citrine," "Garnet"
Big Pulp	"Star Sapphire"
Black Lantern	"Copal"
Blast Furnace	"Ivory"
The Brownstone Poets 2012 Anthology, ed. Patricia Carragon (New York City: Patricia Carragon, 2012)	"Aquamarine"
Buddhist Poetry Review	"Padparadscha"
Danse Macabre	"Opal," "White Topaz"
Danse Macabre du Jour	"Doublet"
"Divine Intimacy," ed. Bobbi Dykema, PhD	"Nephrite"
Eye to the Telescope	"Lodestone"
Green Briar Review	"Emerald"
Iambs & Trochees	"Coral," "Spinel"
Impractical Cats, eds. Æleen Frisch and Patricia Flint (Wallingford, CT: Medusa's Laugh Press, 2013)	"Cat's Eye"
Oyez Review	"Cubic Zirconium"
Penguin Review	"Onyx"
Up the Staircase Quarterly	"Created Sapphire"

VQ	"Helenite"
The Waiting Room Reader II, ed. Rachel Hadas (Fort Lee, NJ: CavanKerry Press, 2013)	"Bloodstone"

"Marble" also appeared under the title "Venus De Milo" in *Heavenly Bodies* (Hoboken, NJ: Poets Wear Prada, 2008).

"Diamond" was published as a limited edition micro-chap by Poets Wear Prada in 2012, and nominated for a 2013 Pushcart Prize.

The author would also like to gratefully acknowledge William Butler Yeats's poem "Lapis Lazuli" as the source and inspiration for the author's poem of the same title.

About the Author

Related to the Marx Brothers through his mother, Richard Marx Weinraub was born in New York City in 1949. He was a Professor of English at the University of Puerto Rico from 1987 through 2010. A book of his poetry entitled *Wonder Bread Hill* was published in 2002 by the University of Puerto Rico Press. Poets Wear Prada published his chapbook *Heavenly Bodies* in 2008, and a poem from it was nominated for a 2009 Pushcart Prize. His poetry has appeared in many journals including *The Paris Review, Asheville Poetry Review, South Carolina Review, The Hampden-Sydney Poetry Review, Green Mountains Review, North American Review, Slate,* and *River Styx.*

www.ingramcontent.com/pod-product-compliance
Lightning Source LLC
Chambersburg PA
CBHW031213090426
42736CB00009B/904